KIDDING AROUND

New York City

A YOUNG PERSON'S GUIDE TO THE CITY

SARAH LOVETT

ILLUSTRATED BY SALLY BLAKEMORE

John Muir Publications
Santa Fe, New Mexico

City Tips—Have a grown-up with you at all times. Even kids who spend their whole lives in the city don't wander around alone. If you get lost, find the nearest uniformed NYPD officer, uniformed guard, or information desk. For emergencies (fire, first aid, accidents, ambulance, or police), dial 911. And most of all, ***don't panic!***

Special thanks to Eda Gordon, Steven Schmidt, Chris McPartland, Ylise Kessler, Peter Winslow, and Suzi Winson, Ian Woodard, Alex Simon, Mia Flato and all the other kids.

Alice, Amber, and Jade Sealey

John Muir Publications, P.O. Box 613, Santa Fe, NM 87504

First edition. First printing

Library of Congress Cataloging-in-Publication Data

Lovett, Sarah, 1953-
    Kidding around New York City: a young person's guide to the city/Sarah Lovett; illustrated by Sally Blakemore.—1st ed.
        p.   cm.
    Summary: Describes sights and events of interest in New York City, including lower Manhattan, the midtown area, and the other boroughs.
        ISBN 0-945465-33-5
        1. New York (N.Y.)—Description—1981- —Guide-books—Juvenile literature. 2. Children—Travel—New York (N.Y.)—Guide-books—Juvenile literature. [1. New York (N.Y.)—Description—Guides.] I. Blakemore, Sally, ill. II. Title.
F128.18.L69   1989
917.47'10443—dc20   89-42936
                                                    CIP
                                                    AC

Typeface: Trump Medieval
Typesetter: Copygraphics, Santa Fe, New Mexico
Designer: Joanna V. Hill
Printer: Eurasia Press

Distributed to the book trade by:
W.W. Norton & Company, Inc.
New York, New York

Contents

1. A Bite of the Big Apple

New York City, the "Big Apple," is hustle-bustle, flash and sparkle, and lots of energy! More than seven million people call it home. They work in skyscrapers and tunnels, they commute on subways and ferry boats, and they live in neighborhoods as varied from one another and unique as knishes, moo shu pork, and gelato.

It's no accident that the Statue of Liberty stands on Liberty Island at the entrance to New York harbor. Since her unveiling in 1886, she has welcomed millions of immigrants to the "new world" with her promise of justice and freedom.

The first inhabitants of what is now New York City were Native Americans who trapped, fished, planted, and lived a fairly peaceful tribal life. (Wow, have things ever changed!)

Since those early times, Germans, Irish, Italians, West Indians, Latin Americans, Asians, and many others have crossed the oceans to settle in New York City's neighborhoods. The result is a wonderful explosion of people, sights, and sounds. From Little Italy and Chinatown in Lower Manhattan to German Yorkville on the East Side and Harlem just north of Central

The Big Apple got its name from musicians in the 1920s and 30s who sang, "Hey man, there are plenty of apples on the tree, but I'm playing New York City! I've made it to the big time. I've made it to the Big Apple!"

Park—you can sample all these different worlds in one city.

The island of Manhattan (where most people visit) is only part of the apple pie. Officially, there are five boroughs that make up New York City. Besides Manhattan, there's Queens, Brooklyn, the Bronx, and Richmond (or Staten Island). Each borough offers something special—like the Bronx Zoo, the Brooklyn Botanical Garden, the New York Hall of Science in Queens, and the Staten Island Children's Museum.

Now that you know the basics, get ready, get set, to take your bite of the big apple!

Circumnavigating the Big Apple—The easiest way to get around NYC is in a great pair of walking shoes. Subways are cheap, and be prepared for lots of local color. The subway trains themselves aren't bad, but the stations can be smelly, dirty, and damp. Take a taxicab and you'll meet cabbies from all over the world. Buses are clean and a great way to see the city, and you can transfer.

2. Apple Maps

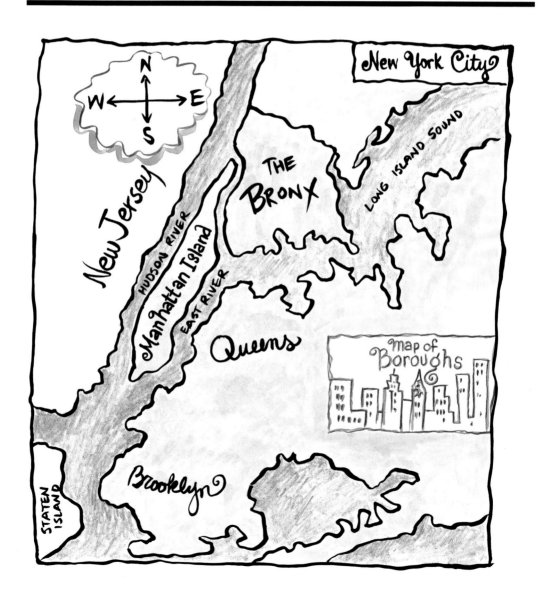

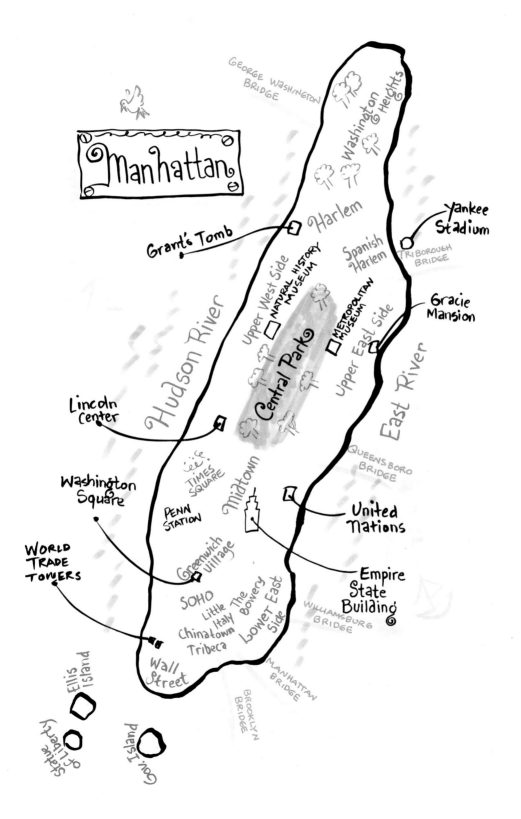

3. Apple Time

The Algonquin and other Indian tribes inhabit what is now New York City.

1524-Giovanni da Verrazano explores New York bay.

1609-Henry Hudson sails his ship, the *Half Moon*, up what is now the Hudson River. He's exploring for the Dutch East India Company.

1626-Peter Minuit, working for the Dutch West India Company, "buys" Manhattan from the Indians for $24 in trinkets.

1664-The English take over New Amsterdam and call it New York after the Duke of York, brother to King Charles II of England.

1775 to 1783-The War of Independence, or American Revolution. George Washington commands troops around New York fighting the British.

1785-New York City briefly becomes the capital of the U.S.

1789-The U.S. Constitution is ratified and General George Washington becomes the first president.

1807-Robert Fulton christens his steamboat, the *Clermont*, on the Hudson.

1835-The Great Fire burns down much of New York's business district.

1853-New York hosts the World's Fair.

1886-Statue of Liberty is inaugurated.

1898-Greater New York, all five boroughs, is created.

1900-A population of more than 3 million makes New York the largest city in the world!

1902-The Flatiron Building, one of the first skyscrapers in New York, is erected.

1904-Subway first opened.

1931-Empire State Building completed.

1945-United Nations charter drafted.

1964 to 1965-New York is the site of the World's Fair once again.

1969-A Ticker Tape Parade honors the first astronauts to land on the moon.

1973-The World Trade Center opens.

1975-New York goes wild with the American Bicentennial celebrations.

1986-Statue of Liberty is one hundred years old and has a party!

4. A View from the Top (Lower Manhattan)

BOO! In the mood to bust a ghost? Try haunting the NYC Fire Department's Ladder Co. #8 (10–14 N. Moore St. and Varick). It's a real fire station, and it's also the location of the ghostbusting offices. Other film locations include the NY Public Library and the Tavern on the Green. Don't get slimed!

et's start with Manhattan. Remember it's an island surrounded by the Hudson River, the East River, New York Bay, and the Harlem River. Even though Manhattan is only 13.4 miles lengthwise and at its widest point just 2.3 miles across, it's filled with things to see and do. So we'll begin at the bottom, and that means the nine neighborhoods of lower Manhattan.

One of the first places to explore in all of New York City is right here. **The World Trade Center (WTC)**, or twin towers, stands on 16 acres in lower Manhattan. On the ground floor, you'll find restaurants, flower stands, bookstores, drugstores, and banks. In fact, it's a mini-city. But don't waste any time. You want to get to the top! An escalator takes you to the ticket booth where visibility is posted. If it's "zero," don't go up unless you enjoy weird experiences like standing around in gray fuzz. But let's hope you're lucky. Even five- or ten-mile visibility will blow your mind. The elevator is a thrill in itself. Packed in like sardines, you get to listen to the wind howl down the elevator shaft like a ghost afraid of heights. The trip to the top of the world takes about 58 seconds. Try running up the stairs **that** fast.

The World Trade Center offers the world's highest open-air promenade—110 stories up. On crystal-clear days, you can see 55 miles in every direction. Pick out the Brooklyn Bridge, Queensboro Bridge, Roosevelt Island, Little Italy, New Jersey, and Ellis Island. If it's too cold or windy and the promenade is closed, you'll get an equally good view on the Deck, three floors down and a quarter mile high! If heights make you dizzy or green, look down anyway. You can sit on the metal benches and the glass is thick. You really won't fall through. A sunset view is romantic (if you go in for that kind of stuff). It's a view like no other in the world.

Battery Park City, right across from the WTC, is new and shiny and filled with shops, restaurants, parks, and plazas. You'd hardly guess this city within a city is built on 92 acres of landfill, which is a polite word for trash. Since cities are crowded and garbage is plentiful, does it make sense to recycle our trash, then bury what's left over and build on top? Stroll along the esplanade and wave at New Jersey directly across the harbor. After you do your shopping and eating, make a stop at **Winter Garden**. All that vaulted glass is amazing, and the palm trees give you a taste of the tropics.

Another way to get your bearings in the Big Apple is on deck beginning at Pier 83. **Circle Line** cruises head down the Hudson River every 30 to 45 minutes (in season), and you'll pass the World Trade Center, the Statue of Liberty, and Ellis Island. Turn the corner up the East River and look up at the Brooklyn Bridge, Manhattan Bridge, and Williamsburg Bridge. Watch out for a stiff neck. By now you've passed Chinatown on the left and Brooklyn on the right. After the

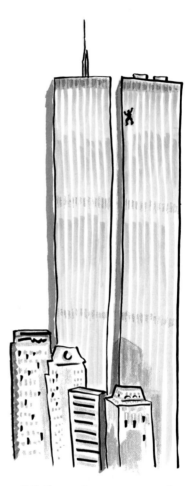

While you're up on top of the World Trade Center, try to imagine yourself as the "human fly." A few years ago he scaled the WTC using suction cups and expanders. These days there are special barriers to keep would-be "flies" from doing their thing and upsetting the SWAT team.

Living on an island has its own special problems. What do you do with all your trash? In New York, trash is used for landfill (like Battery Park) or hauled out to sea and dumped. The problem with that is it sinks to the bottom and forms a gooey gunk and ocean currents push it back into shore. So now the trash barges cruise farther out to sea before they dump their trash. Unfortunately, what to do with garbage is still a problem. So recycle!

United Nations Headquarters, look back to the right and hope the Delacorte Geyser is doing its thing. It's a natural fountain, and every once in a while, it shoots water as high as 400 feet into the air. As you pass under the Queensboro Bridge, check out the 59th Street Tramway hooking up Roosevelt Island with Manhattan. The island used to be a prison without walls. The riptides were so strong that no prisoner ever survived escape. Farther upstream (by now you're on the Harlem River), you can spot Yankee Stadium in the Bronx and turn the corner again onto the Hudson. Pass the Cloisters, George Washington Bridge, and Grant's Tomb, and you're almost docked again at 43rd Street.

Back on dry ground, **Battery Park** is the place to feed a squirrel and imagine what **Castle Clinton** was like in 1811 or 1812 when it was built to defend New York harbor from British attack.

Well, not a single shot was ever fired from the fort, and since then it's been a performance space, an immigration station, the city's aquarium, and now a national monument. When Castle Clinton served as an immigration depot between 1855 and 1890, 8 million people entered the United States through its gateway. Many of the immigrants during those years were of Irish, German, and Jewish descent and settled in the neighborhoods you're visiting.

Castle Clinton is also where you catch the ferry to **Liberty Island** and the Statue of you-know-who! The trip to the island lasts only a few minutes. But take the time to think about what you're about to see. **The Statue of Liberty** symbolizes a free and just world for all people. Her 100th anniversary was in 1986, and New York went wild with celebration. You'll see why. She's 152 feet high on a pedestal that's 150 feet high. Depending on the crowds, it can take anywhere from 20 minutes (moving fast!) to 3 hours to climb the 344 steps to Liberty's crown. The smaller you are, the better, because it's tight going, especially for the last six or seven flights. Also, you're going in a spiral, so you might get dizzy. Once you're there, it's worth the effort. You can feel yourself sway in the winds as you check out the view from the crown. Look out at the harbor and imagine what it must have been like for the millions of immigrants who braved months of ocean hardship to reach America. The torch, standing for freedom and justice, must have been an amazing sight—America! For less athletic types (like parents), there's the elevator to the observation deck and another great view.

The **American Museum of Immigration** located in the base of the statue gives you a taste

Standing in line for the ferry to Liberty Island gives you the opportunity to examine all the strange souvenirs being hawked. Can you figure out what these impromptu entrepreneurs are saying? "Heep and getter oree ginl ott-chirt! Nnnnnnly siz ninny fiv!"

*At Pier 86, just upriver from where the Circle Line docks, step on board the **Intrepid Sea-Air-Space Museum** (a real W.W. II aircraft carrier). You can watch films, get the feel of a real jetfighter, or examine models of space capsules.*

of what people went through to reach America. Some were slaves, others fled political or religious oppression, and some just dreamed of a new and better life for their families. At the museum, take the time to consider how important it is to have a home, family, and country you believe in.

Outside, on the promenade, you can drop a quarter in the observation binoculars and review your landmarks. See if you can pick out Verrazano Bridge where the New York Marathon starts each year.

Grrrrrrr! If hunger strikes you on Liberty Island, you better like fast food. Burgers, cokes, fries, and plenty of grease are available in the snack bar. (It also helps to have an iron stomach!)

Staten Island Ferry offers you the best deal in town. For a quarter (yes, that's 25 cents!), you can ride to Staten Island and back again. It's a great time for people-watching (or stargazing at night). But things have changed in the last few years because of the homeless. In the Ferry Terminal, waiting for the next boat, you can't help but notice the folks who use the benches as beds and temporary shelter from the streets outside. New York City, like all big cities, has lots and lots of homeless people. Some of them are sick, others used to own homes or rent apartments but lost their jobs and money from hard luck. Sometimes we seem to forget that homeless people are not eyesores to be ignored but fellow human beings caught in a social dilemma that demands a solution.

On board the ferry, keep an eye out for tugboats trudging barges against the tide, fish, birds, and buoys. You can get a shoeshine (unless you're

Chances are, you know someone who's great-great-grandparents, great-aunts, or great-uncles landed on **Ellis Island** anywhere from 1892 to 1954. Just like Castle Clinton, Ellis Island was an immigration depot. At least ten million immigrants were processed—and sometimes that meant they were given a new name—before they could land on Manhattan. Now Ellis Island is a museum open to the public and definitely worth a visit.

*All hands on deck! The deck of the **Pioneer**, that is. If it's spring or summer, **South Street Seaport** offers you the chance to try out your sea legs. Back in the 1800s South Street was a bustling seaport and the shipping capital of the New World. These days, there's lots to see and do for a nautical flash from the past. Don't miss a stroll on board the* Peking, *a steel four-masted bark. The second-largest sailing ship in the world, she dates back to 1911 and you can find her anchored at Pier 16.*

wearing Nikes) or buy a snack. Menus vary from burritos to egg rolls and knishes and cracker-jacks. If the weather's good, make sure you stand up front in the open air and listen to a musician or two. Once you reach Staten Island, it's fine to turn right around and enjoy the spectacular view of Manhattan.

After you disembark from the Liberty Island Ferry, take a walk over to the **Vietnam Veterans Memorial**. It's 16 feet high and 70 feet long. This glass and brick sculpture is there to remind us of the Vietnam War and all the men and women who died in it. There are poems, letters, and news reports etched in the glass. While you're reading, take some time to think about how countries can learn to work out their differences without fighting. After all, that's exactly what you do every day with the people around you.

5. Bulls, Bears, and Billions

ew York City still boasts the title of the world's money capital. And Wall Street is where lots of "invisible" monies (or securities) change hands. But Wall Street is more than a street, it's a district and a way of life. If people tell you they work on Wall Street, they might mean Cedar, William, or Pine Street. And chances are they're brokers, specialists, or clerks.

Wall Street has a colorful and volatile history. In 1653, a municipal government was established in Nieuw Amsterdam and the council ordered the rebuilding of an old wall along the southern tip of Manhattan Island. Originally used as protection from the Indians, the wall was fortified to hold off English aggressors. The English still managed to defeat the Dutch and rename Nieuw Amsterdam New York. And speaking of names. . . now you know how Wall Street got its name.

After the Revolutionary War, the states were left with $80,000,000 worth of debts, and the first Congress voted to issue bonds—paper certificates that are sort of like government I.O.U.'s. When all the bonds were sold, people began to resell them to each other. They did lots of trading and selling in coffeehouses and it was a little bit crazy. So twenty-four businessmen and traders agreed to meet each day at a specific time and place to do their business—buying and selling securities. They picked a cool, shady spot under a big, old buttonwood tree (wouldn't you?) that grew in the present-day sight of 68 Wall Street. Those guys were the first members of the New York Stock Exchange.

There are a total of seven stock exchanges in the United States. Two of them, the **New York Stock Exchange (NYSE)** and the **American Stock Exchange**, are located within a few blocks of each other. Either one is worth a visit for future financial wizards.

Upstairs, in the Visitors Gallery of the NYSE, learn market jargon like "selling short" and "liquid stock." (Just think how you can amaze and confuse your friends.) Computer monitors offer dictionary definitions and a six-minute film gives you an overview. But the real entertainment is the observation deck that overlooks the floor of the exchange itself. A recorded message (in many languages) explains what the

*Even though you won't see all 1,366 members on the floor of the **NYSE**, you'll see lots of ticker tape and plenty of hubbub and ruckus.*

frantic action is all about. Who knows? Maybe soon, you'll be a broker wheeling and dealing some of the millions of shares traded daily.

Up the block from the NYSE, drop in at **Federal Hall National Memorial** built in 1842. This site marks many moments in history. The first Congress convened on this very spot. Eight weeks later, on April 30, 1789, General George Washington was inaugurated as the first president of the United States amidst cheering crowds outside Federal Hall. Step inside, take a look at the rotunda, and check out the **Federal Hall Memorial Museum**. You can pick up the Bill of Rights that Congress adopted here, or a deed to the Statue of Liberty. But don't try to take the Statue of Liberty home because the deeds are only copies. You can also buy ink and a quill pen similiar to the one used to write the Declaration of Independence.

On weekdays, if you stroll by **City Hall** on Broadway, you're likely to see the red carpet rolled out. Maybe a movie star or a foreign dignitary is visiting. In that case, there will be lots of handshakes and flashbulbs. Since City Hall is the office of the mayor of New York, you might even see the "big man" himself. He's the official greeter for the city as well as an administrator of city policy. City Hall is a landmark (built between 1803 and 1811), and it's also a beautiful building. In fact, it's considered one of the most beautiful in the United States. There's also a museum where you can see George Washington's desk as well as other relics of early America.

The **Woolworth Building** across the street has an eye-stopping lobby and the outside's "gotta" be Gothic.

The **New York Stock Exchange** is your chance to see Bull and Bear action. These are market terms. Bullish means people think prices are rising and there's money to be made. Bearish isn't so positive—might mean getting bummed out.

In 1733, John Peter Zenger attacked the governor of New York in his weekly paper. The Royal Governor, William Cosby, was particularly upset by some raucous anti-Cosby poems. Zenger was imprisoned in City Hall (Federal Hall) for slander and his writing burned in the streets. After nine months in prison, his acquittal marked the beginning of freedom of the press.

If you're hungry for food and history, drop by **Fraunces Tavern** on Pearl Street. After all, George Washington did. That's where he gave his farewell speech to his officers on December 4, 1783, at the end of the American Revolution.

Now the tavern is a museum of American history and a restaurant to boot. You'll see permanent and changing exhibits about the Revolutionary War and life in the 1700s. Ask about the slide shows and lectures if you're in the mood. And make sure you order baked chicken à la Washington in the restaurant on the ground floor. It's the oldest continuously operated restaurant in the entire United States!

On Water Street at Peck Slip between Front and South streets, examine the fake Brooklyn Bridge painted on the side of Consolidated Edison's power station. The mural, by Richard Haas, won a prize. Don't let your eyes fool you with the real bridge in the background.

It's not every day that you get to stand and stare at $800,000,000 worth of gold bars within arm's reach. But a visit to the **Federal Reserve** on Liberty Street gives you a glimpse at more gold than you can find in Fort Knox! Of course, there are steel bars between you and all that money, so don't get carried away with the Midas touch.

Think of the Federal Reserve as a big bank for little banks. If you pass a bank or savings and loan on any street in New York City, chances are they have an account with the Federal Reserve. When they need to make a deposit they send money over in armored cars. They make withdrawals, too.

The Federal Reserve Bank of New York processes about 7,000,000 currency bills each day (that's about $120 million in case you wondered).

Out of all those bills, about $40 million get shredded into 35 strips each because they're too old and funky. On the free one-hour tour, you'll get your own souvenir shreds. If you could put them back together, you'd have about $5.00. Good luck.

Down on E level, about 50 feet below sea level, is where you'll find the largest supply of gold in the free world. Only a fraction of the gold is owned by the United States. All the rest is in top-secret accounts from other nations. About 900,000 individual gold bars are stored behind a 90-ton steel cylinder that rotates in a 140-ton steel frame. That's the only way in. The largest compartment holds about 107,000 gold bricks. Imagine a wall of solid gold 15 feet tall and 18 feet thick. Just one of those golden bars could cover your allowance for the rest of your life.

*The **Federal Reserve** holds over 10,000 tons of gold. Each gold bar weighs about 400 troy ounces or 27 avoirdupois pounds!*

21

6. Holograms and Walking Potatoes

There's still lot's more eye-popping sights downtown. Greenwich Village, the East Village, Soho, and TriBeCa are filled with trendy galleries and restaurants, chichi shops, and artist's studios. (Keep in mind that the trendiest hot spots often look like they were recently bombed and burned. That just means they're very expensive.) If all that chic is a yawn, just step outside for entertainment. The streets are filled with action. You're as likely to see a unicyclist juggling flaming tomatoes, a movie star, or a giant potato on foot as you are regular old human beings. You'll be on foot, too, because downtown streets are made for walking.

The first thing you might wonder when you find **Greenwich Village** (if you find it!) is who planned this hodgepodge of streets. Nobody. It just sort of happened. At one time Greenwich

*"UJO" (Unidentified Jumping Object). Long jumps over ten human "volunteers" have been unofficially reported in **Washington Square Park**. Six unicyclists were also spotted with electric light bulbs glowing from their hairdos.*

Village was an Algonquin Indian village. After the Dutch settled in Nieuw Amsterdam, the area became a tobacco plantation. Since it was green and "wich" is a Saxon (very early English) word for village, it was a "green village." But today it's asphalt, concrete, nineteenth-century houses, shops of all types, and restaurants. If people tell you to check out "the Village," this is what they mean. The boundaries of Greenwich Village are Houston (pronounced like a ton of houses) to the south, 14th Street to the north, somewhere between Broadway and Lafayette on the east, and Hudson Street to the west. Roughly in the center of that trapezoidal chunk of geography sits **Washington Square**. In the 1700s, Washington Square was a field where thousands of plague victims and poor folks were buried. Public executions were also held here. When it was renovated years ago, 10,000 skeletons were dug up! Make no bones about it, that's a lot of clavicles and femurs. Later it was a drill ground for soldiers. Now the park is the center of much live action on days when the sun shines. New York University is located right here and you'll see students galore. The park isn't a place to visit by yourself, but hang out with friends or family, dodge the skateboarders, and watch the magicians, jugglers, and plain old weirdos do their thing.

In the 1930s, Greenwich Village was a Bohemian center. Artists and writers came from all over the world to experience the Village and all that it meant: new, fringe, experimental. Today, trends blow by so fast it seems like nothing is new. What's a nonconformist to do? Being different isn't easy, but it's really important. "Different" folks are the pioneers who break new ground and "go where no person has dared go before." Yikes!

ASTOR PLACE
HAIR CUTS

*If you need to change your locks, then **Astor Place Hair Designers** is still the place to get buzzed, snipped, spiked, neoned, or kinked. But your grown-up may never speak to you again.*

Do wander around the Village, and do plan to get lost. Streets crisscross like a bunch of pickup sticks. Also keep in mind that Avenue of the Americas is really Sixth Avenue. That's what New Yorkers call it and you should, too. **Urban Outfitters**, not far from Washington Square, is where you'll find clothes and kitsch. You might want to stop for a bite at **The Penguin Cafe** or sit outside at the **White Horse Tavern**, both on Hudson. If you're cruising along Broadway, pop into **Tower Records** when you get to 4th Street. Whatever kind of music you enjoy, they'll play your tune. It's also a hangout for local kids.

When Greenwich Village became too expensive for artists to afford, they moved right next door to the **East Village**. Boundaries here are Houston Street, the East River on the east (where else?), 14th Street to the north, and Bowery on the west. For a street scene in the East Village, you can visit St. Mark's Place, Astor Place, and Lafayette Street. Some parts of the East Village aren't very hospitable. Keep a grown-up handy at all times.

Lafayette Street boasts the **Public Theatre** (started by Joseph Papp), where the shows are plentiful and not too expensive, and **Astor Place Theatre**. Both are big deals in the Off-Broadway theater scene. If you're a theater-o-phile, rehearse current production schedules and buy yourself a ticket.

Just a block away, pop into the **Astor Place subway station**. It was spiffed up in recent history and it's worth a peek.

Star Magic, on Broadway near Astor Place, will beam you up with spacey gadgets, scientific instruments, books, minerals, and plenty of future shocks in stock.

St. Mark's Place (where 8th St. continues between First and Third avenues) is the main street in the East Village. You'll find some great stores like **Trash & Vaudeville** and eateries like **Cafe Orlin**. Great for shopping, noshing, or just poking around.

What is south of Houston, chockablock with galleries, and wacky on weekends? **Soho!** That's the area (26 blocks) between Houston Street, Canal Street, Sixth Avenue (remember it's not Ave. of the Americas), and Lafayette Street. Once again, you'll find galleries, restaurants, and shops where arty types hang out. Soho really boomed in the late 1950s and 1960s when the artists

Cooper Union for the Advancement of Science and Art, on Astor Place, was founded in 1859. Peter Cooper wanted to start a college so poor boys could get an education. (What about poor girls?) Stop a moment if you're passing by. Here, in 1860, Abraham Lincoln gave a speech about slavery that helped him get elected president. Joseph Campbell, an expert on myths who died recently, lectured a few years back. Those lectures were the inspiration for the movie Star Wars. The point is you never know what your words will inspire!

New York City Kids—How do you think they're different from you? Are they more sophisticated or more protected? How is growing up in a city different from growing up in your town? If a friend came to visit you from New York, what would you show them?

moved into warehouses and lofts. If you're interested in architecture, look down, up, and around. This area has the world's biggest concentration of historic cast-iron buildings dating from 1850 to 1880. Take a magnet along to test for the real thing.

When you visit Soho, go on a weekend for the best people-watching and don't arrive before noon. Start on West Broadway because that's the liveliest Soho street. But Wooster, Spring, Mercer, and Broome streets all offer surprises.

If you're into fashion trends, don't miss **Parachute** (Wooster). It resembles a concrete bunker, and it's great just to look at and imagine the future when snobby cyborgs croak, "May I help you find your style?"

Your basic clothes stores include **Canal Jean Co**. (on Broadway), **American High** (W. Broadway), and **Betsey Johnson** (Thompson St.).

If you don't need duds, but you're in the mood for something special, **Think Big** (W. Broadway between Spring and Broome). It's a store where, you guessed it, everything is larger than life. You might find a light bulb the size of a chair, a seven-foot-high pencil, or a safety pin that will fit on your head. It's filled with everything you just can't live without. Or get lost in the **Enchanted Forest** on Mercer Street near Spring Street where you can enter a crystal cave that will transform you several times. The "forest" was created by a theatrical set designer. And you'll find toys, books, gems, and whimsies. It's magic.

But don't spend all your time shopping. It's time to get weird! **The Museum of Holography** on Mercer near Canal Street is filled with fabulous holograms of gremlins, crocodiles, and eerie human heads. You'll learn about the properties of lightwaves that crest and trough and vary according to color. Holograms are made with lasers, but the position of laser beams, objects, lights, and emulsion make for big differences. You'll understand all this and more after viewing the 20-minute video that plays every hour on the half-hour. And you can buy some nifty souvenir holograms at the gift shop.

While you're in the "off-the-wall" museum mood, don't miss the **Museum of Colored Glass and Light** (On Wooster St. near Spring St.). On display are all the creations of Raphael Nemeth, a friendly and gentle man who gladly answers questions. It might remind you of a church because the glass artworks are a little like stained glass, but the subjects include presidents, circuses, and soda bottles. Mr. Nemeth created his own process with lots of imagination and now he has his own museum. If you were going to start your own museum, what would you put inside?

Last but not least, explore the triangle below Canal Street. That's the area called **TriBeCa**. More artists?! Yes, there are artists who live here, too. In fact, this is the most recent area for an artists' takeover. But besides cafés, galleries, and warehouses you'll find great radio/TV components around Church or Reade Street. Electronic wizards will get a charge from all the wild wiring, circuit boards, and oscilloscopes that let you see radio waves on screen.

The New York City Fire Museum displays shiny red fire engines and other tools of the firefighting trade. If you've ever dreamed of sliding down a pole and answering the call for help or saving babies from raging infernos, this is the place for you.

7. Bird Brains and Cannoli

Lower Manhattan, or downtown, is where the city of New York began. Everyone seemed to settle right here. Later, the city expanded north to accommodate all of them. Three more neighborhoods downtown absolutely must be visited.

Close your eyes and the thought of Chinatown might conjure up visions of opium dens and dragon ladies. But that's the stuff of Saturday matinees at the mall. Take a walk along any of the dozen square blocks of the real Chinatown and you'll be impressed by the crowds, the window displays, and the thrill of being in another world.

This area has a population of more than 100,000, which explains why it feels so crowded. You'll notice an exotic combination of tenement buildings crowned with gilded pagodas and red dragons.

If you start at Chatham Square and cross the street where Mott and Worth streets meet, you're entering Chinatown. The first stop is on your right, #8 Mott Street, where you'll find the **Chinatown Fair** video arcade and the "world famous" **Bird Brain**. Yes, kids, for 50 cents you can play Tic Tac Toe with a live chicken.

Chances are she'll beat the pants off you. A "Bird Brain" is what you'll feel like after just one game! There's also a live dancing chicken, but she may or may not be out of order. By the way, this arcade offers regular old video games, too, if you need a techtronic fix.

Keep walking and you'll bump into Bayard Street and the **Original Chinatown Ice Cream Factory**. They've been in business for about ten years. Tempt your tongue with flavors like Litchi, Green Tea, Chrysanthemum, Ginger, and Red Bean. But if you're absolutely dying for Oreo Cookie flavor, they've got that, too.

Back on Mott Street, you'll find one of twelve **Buddhist temples** located in Chinatown. Visitors are welcome, and the candlelit shrine is a bright sight under the colorful Chinese lanterns and banners. (If you see many bottles of Mazola Oil, it's for the candles.) For a small donation you can pick up your fortune and a touch of good luck at the same time. All in English. Sit for a while and quietly watch.

This chicken isn't any old fowl. In fact, she's appeared on Eye-Witness News and That's Incredible. If you win at Tic Tac Toe (fat chance), you can munch on Chinese fortune cookies for a lifetime.

29

Chinese New Year is celebrated on the first full moon after January 19. The streets are filled with thousands of people, and firecrackers fall through the air like rain. It's a wild and noisy experience. Even the New York policemen and policewomen wear earplugs. If you go, plug up and get ready to duck for cover!

Fung Wong Bakery on Mott Street offers authentic pastries and bakery goods prepared by traditional Chinese methods. And it's big!

On the corner of Bayard Street, step inside **Dried Beef King** for a taste of dried oyster beef or curry beef, a Chinese treat. If you're a vegetarian, try Dried Plum, Preserved Lemon, Ginseng Cured Prune, or hard and chewy rice candy displayed like colored confetti.

Now you're right next door to **Columbus Park**. Recently renovated, it's a nice place to take a break from all the hubbub.

For a taste treat, sample a little dim sum (those bite-sized delicacies), lo mein, or mu gai pan. Order Bird's Nest Soup made from a real bird's nest. Or if you really want to spice up your tongue, go Szechuan!

If you could close your eyes and suddenly beam yourself three blocks north to Mulberry Street, the sounds and smells would be completely different. You don't hear the staccato of Chinese being spoken. And you don't smell stir fry and firecrackers. Open your eyes and you're standing in the middle of **Little Italy**. There used to be mulberry trees growing all around here, but no more. See the salami hanging from the ceilings of the meat shops. Notice the endless bundles of pasta of every possible shape.

Look for the bright sign of **Ferrara's** on Grand Street. It's been here since 1892 and you'll taste why. You better warn your sweet tooth about cannoli, a pastry with a sweet filling almost like frosting. There are over 20 different types of pastries to choose from, so go wild. Grown-ups can refuel with tasty cafe latte or cappucino.

Each year in early September, Mulberry Street becomes a huge carnival with games, music, and calzone, sausage, and zeppole for bigger than bite-sized diversion. All this happens in honor of **San Gennaro**. *He was born in Naples, Italy, and he died in 305. The story says he was thrown to wild beasts who refused to harm him so he was beheaded instead. His day is September 19.*

In 1910, a stroll down a street on the **Lower East Side** would take you into teeming crowds of immigrants, tenement buildings, awning-covered meat and vegetable stands, children playing in streets and gutters, and vendors calling their wares in every language except English. Italian, Irish, and Jewish families shared the area between Canal Street to the south and Seventh Street to the north. There was a lot going on in those days. And there still is today, even though it's different.

The place to learn about immigrants (maybe even your great-grandparents) is the **Lower East Side Tenement Museum**. Exhibits change frequently. You might follow a costumed actor on a tour of the neighborhoods or watch a play about a turn-of-the-century family.

While Saturday is the Jewish Sabbath (holy day), on Sundays **Orchard Street** is the hot spot for bright-eyed bargain hunters. You'll find petticoats, can openers, shoelaces, and knickers. Make sure you barter. That means, if the merchant says it costs five dollars, you say, "Would you take two-fifty?" They say, "Four!" You boldly smack your three dollars down on the table. "Three is my rock bottom offer!" And maybe you just bought yourself a glow-in-the-dark lava lamp.

8. King Kong and the General Assembly (Midtown Manhattan)

idtown Manhattan feels very different from downtown. For one thing, it's not as narrow or old. The top of midtown is bordered by Central Park. The rivers mark the boundaries on east and west and the southern end is 34th Street and guess what building?

Now you can venture up, up, up inside one of the eight wonders of the world, the **Empire State Building** on Fifth Avenue, also called the world's largest Christmas tree. In 1931, when it was built on what was once the site of a great fishing hole for eel and sunfish, it was the world's tallest building. You've probably seen King Kong's "last stand" on the late, late show. Fortunately, you won't have to fight off all the artillery.

The Empire State Building has 6,500 windows to wash and contains 60,000 tons of steel. You can take the art deco elevators up to the 86th floor observation deck (1,050 feet up) or continue up to the 102nd floor observatory (1,250 feet up). On a clear day you won't see forever but almost—as far as 80 miles. If you wanted to walk to the top from the ground floor, it would only take you 1,860 steps! Think about that twice.

Now that you've been up, head down to the

See how you measure up to the world's tallest man at 8 feet, 11.1 inches, or the world's fattest, smallest, or longest at Guinness Book of World Records.

*Check out the **Flatiron Building** where Broadway crosses Fifth Avenue at 23rd Street.*

Photo courtesy of New York Convention & Visitors Bureau

Guinness World of Records. Sports trivia fans should make a home run for the World of Sports data banks for football, baseball, and soccer records. Geologists and astronauts can beeline it to the Natural World/Space Achievements. And connoisseurs of the weird and gross will be fascinated by the video of a man devouring 32 eggs in 78 seconds, 144 prunes in 32 seconds, or 250 oysters in 2 minutes and 52.33 seconds. There's something for almost everyone.

Speaking of biggest and best, **Macy's and Co**. holds the title of world's largest department store. Some experts say Macy's toy department is a great spot to shop. If you like 'em big, why not check it out for yourself? It's right across the street between Seventh and Broadway.

The Chrysler Building on Lexington Avenue and 42nd Street glows day or night. Its tower (reaching 1,048 feet into the air) made it the world's tallest building. . .for a few weeks. Then the Empire State Building was completed and the spire added on top to outdo Chrysler. The Chrysler Building really is beautiful. See if you can pick out "car parts" in the design.

The **United Nations** was started in 1945 to solve disputes between nations, peaceably! World War II (1939-1945) was the worst war in the history of this planet. Millions of people died and the world was devastated by the horrors of what did happen and the thought that it might happen again. On August 14, 1945, America dropped the first atomic bombs on Hiroshima and Nagasaki in Japan. Although the war was finally over, the new weapons made the possibility of future wars even more unthinkable. Out of this fear, nations first began to think of uniting for purposes of world security.

When you visit the U.N. (on 42nd St. and the East River), be sure to take the tour. It's only an hour long and it's really worth it. Ask your guide how many languages he or she speaks. You may also be surprised that the people in your group come from all over the world.

On the tour there's a display of everyday items like a wristwatch and a baby's shoe that were recovered from Hiroshima after the atomic blast. It's really scary to think about war and death. But we can't hide from the threat of nuclear war. The U.N. reminds us that nations working together can learn to stop fighting.

The Security Council is in charge of maintaining peace throughout the world. It is one of

Don't miss Macy's Parade on Thanksgiving Day! It starts on 77th Street and Central Park West, moves south to Columbus Circle, on to Broadway, and finally to the finish line at Macy's, 34th and Broadway. Fight your way to a curbside seat. Or watch parade preparations the night before. Balloon inflation takes place on Central Park West somewhere between W. 70th and W. 79th.

When you arrive in Manhattan, buy the NY Times *and find the listing of daily UN activities. Better yet, check at the United Nations front desk. There might be an important Council session that you can sit in on!*

several councils that report to the General Assembly, the main organ of the U.N. You'll get to go inside some of the chambers and might even see a council in progress.

If you sit in on a meeting, you'll be wearing headphones that allow you to hear translations in all the official languages—Arabic, Chinese, Spanish, French, Russian, and English.

After the tour take a break in the U.N. cafeteria and browse in all the shops downstairs. If you make reservations ahead of time, it's possible to lunch in the delegates dining room.

The **Horn & Hardart Automat** on 42nd Street is one of the last survivors of a 1930s trend. In those days glass compartments where food is temptingly displayed were considered state-of-the-appetite. You can still feed coins into the slots and "presto"—cherry pie or tuna fish on white bread. A vision of modern times like a Superman comic. This place is fun.

One place you **should** visit during rush hour is

Grand Central Terminal on E. 42nd Street. If you stand on the steps above the central concourse of the terminal, looking down, all those folks running around with briefcases look like zillions of wild ants. More than 170,000 people are said to travel through this terminal daily! After looking down, look up, at the 125-foot-high vaulted ceiling decorated with constellations. It's really a pretty sight. This railroad terminal, a historic landmark, dates back to 1903. Be sure to check out Grand Central's giant clock before you go.

When hunger strikes a chord, hurry on over to the **Hard Rock Cafe** on W. 57th between Broadway and Seventh for a burger, fries, a T-shirt, and lots of noise. Where else do you get to eat under a car crash?

Or try **America** (officially it's lower midtown on E. 18th Street and Fifth Avenue), which seems as big and cavernous as a football stadium and almost as noisy. You can get great P.B.&J., burgers, grilled cheese, or anything else you can possibly think of to eat!

Save your crumbs and take them over to Patience and Fortitude who provide a great pigeon rest stop as they guard the entrance to the NY Public Library. Inside, you'll find great reading, but no crumbs allowed.

*Nibble on bowls of oyster crackers or try a bowl of She Crab soup at the **Oyster Bar Restaurant** in Grand Central Terminal. If you don't want to swallow oysters because you think they're slimy, try the acoustics outside the restaurant under the vaulted ceiling. Someone has to stand opposite you whispering directly into the corner. You should be able to hear every word clearly. It has to do with sound arcs and vibrations.*

9. The Rockettes, Rockefeller, and RCA

Remember Ginger Rogers and Fred Astaire? Nope? Remember Clark Gable and Vivien Leigh? Well, how about the Rockettes? Gee whiz, you must remember something about Radio City Music Hall on Sixth Avenue. This art deco beauty is now an official landmark of New York City and part of Rockefeller Center.

Radio City Music Hall first opened its massive doors in December 1932. America was in the middle of the Great Depression and audiences wanted to "escape into fantasy." They came to Radio City Music Hall and saw extravagant shows with dancers, music, and movies. But through the years, the Music Hall began to lose money and pretty soon it was in very seedy shape. In 1978, it was restored to its original "ritzy" condition, and now theater buffs can see the real stuff that made the magic. Backstage Tours last an hour. If you're into kitch, the bathrooms have wonderful murals and foot-pedal hand driers. If mechanics give you a lift, check out the hydraulic system that was a technological marvel in its day. Military experts came to study the system during World War II as a model for aircraft carriers, but it was off-limits to civilian "spies." Take a peek at the catwalk

(you can look but you "cat" not walk!) if you're not afraid of heights. And cinematic history buffs will appreciate the projection room with giant reels of vintage film.

But that's only a small part of **Rockefeller Center**. You probably know that John D. Rockefeller, Jr., was the son of an oil multimillionaire. In 1929, the year of the great stock market crash, he decided to build a big city within the city of New York. And of course he called it Rockefeller Center! If you find Saks Fifth Avenue, you're right across the street from the **Channel Gardens**, a row of fountains and flowers (that change with the season). At the end of the gardens, you can't miss the Lower Plaza. In the summer, the Lower Plaza is a lovely outdoor

On the tour of Radio City Music Hall, you'll make a stop at the rehearsal hall of the famous synchronized dancers, the Rockettes. If you have visions of kicklines, make sure you measure up to the yardstick on the wall of the hall. If you're under 5'5½" inches or over 5'8½" you're either too short or too tall to make the cut!

*On the **NBC tour** you can practice your "Here's Johnny!" or play the "Tonight Show" host himself in a special mini-studio. You may even see a famous star or two or three!*

café. Ho hum. But in winter, it's a skating rink where you can watch or whizz over the ice.

At the **RCA Building** (still part of the Rockefeller Center), you can take the **NBC Studio** tours where "The Today Show," "Saturday Night Live," and "David Letterman" are recorded. You'll step behind the scenes and learn tidbits of TV production. The Van Go mobile unit gives you the scoop on how those sporting events end up "live" in your living room.

On the 65th floor of the RCA Building, buy your ticket for the Observation Roof and travel via elevator at 16 miles per hour. (Hold onto your stomach!)

The New York Experience surrounds you with cartoons, sound, movies, and multisensory effects of all persuasions. Catch this multimedia extravaganza in the McGraw-Hill Building (yyeessssss! It's part of Rockefeller Center).

The Museum of Modern Art (MOMA), on W. 53rd Street between Fifth and Sixth avenues, rates a stop to see what's on display. The museum boasts two theaters, so check out what films are showing. Spout your opinion on Picasso, Henry Moore, and Andy Warhol and take a rest while you eat in the ground floor cafeteria.

A few paces down the street you'll find a very different type of museum. The archives of the **Museum of Broadcasting** hold more than 10,000 television programs and 10,000 radio programs covering the past 60 years of broadcast history. Radio tapes date from 1920 and television, 1939. You can "check out" Gunsmoke, Howdy Doody, or the Three Stooges for an hour, and three people can fit in for console viewing. While you're there, ask about special workshops and seminars, some just for kids. You might get to make your own fantasy, mystery, or adventure radio show.

A tour of **Carnegie Hall** (on W. 57th St.) gives you an earful of music history. Steel magnate Andrew Carnegie was the benefactor and for 98 years some of the world's greatest musicians have graced the stage of the 2,800-seat hall. Join the likes of Enrico Caruso, Toscanini, Judy Garland, and the Beatles at Carnegie Hall.

Trump Towers, Fifth Avenue and 56th, is awe-inspiring if you go in for glitz, glitter, and gaudy.

Step off Fifth Avenue into the lobby of the **Plaza Hotel.** Flowers, crystal chandeliers, and oriental carpets lead the way to the Palm Court where you can have tea if you're not feeling rowdy. Of course, proper attire is required (that means no torn T-shirts or godzilla masks) and there's an $8 minimum (so make sure someone else has their wallet handy). Look for the portrait of Eloise. She's a famous fictional resident of the Plaza. When you were younger, perhaps you read about her.

Right outside the Plaza Hotel is the place to catch a horse-drawn carriage for a trot around Central Park. It's really fun and the driver might even let you steer if you're very nice.

Rumpelmeyers, right around the corner on Central Park South, a famous ice cream parlor originally founded in Paris in 1860. Sundaes are sweet and pricey.

F.A.O. Schwarz, across the street from the Plaza, is a legend in its own time for kids of every age. You'll find automated trains crossing canyons, bridges, and rivers. Run your fingers over almost life-size race cars (but don't kick the tires). Or Nintendo up and Leggo out.

OK, now for some science you'll love. **AT&T's InfoQuest Center** is recommended by New York kid cognoscenti as "really cool." Located in a tower of the golden AT&T building on 56th and Madison Avenue, InfoQuest starts you off with your own programmed ID card. Throughout the exhibits, use your card to access in and out.

Get the recipe for making microchips or learn about lightguides. You can send zillions of messages through these glass wires, but you can't send your buddy, the neighborhood bully, or your economics teacher. On the way out, don't forget to stop and make your own music video. Pick the star, the costumes, the music, and the look. Look out MTV!

IBM, across the street, has a great atrium for a snack. Then make sure you pop downstairs to see what's on exhibit in the **Gallery of Science and Art**.

St. Patrick's, on Fifth Avenue near 51st Street, is worth a stop. As long as there's no service going on, feel free to quietly enjoy the serenity.

Sci Fi freaks will beam out at **Forbidden Planet** on E. 59th between Second and Third avenues. This great store is loaded with extra(terrestrial)s—classic comic books, fantasy, action gobots, and argonauts.

Broadway means theater! The area (and the street) between 6th Avenue and 8th Avenue near 47th Street (the Times Square area) is chock-full of more than 35 theaters. Catch a musical, drama, or comedy. Whatever you see, it's the same thrill when the curtain rises. TKTS on Broadway and 47th Street is the hot-shop-spot for tickets. Tickets are half-price for same-day shows.

10. Parks and Sharks and the Temple of Dendur (Uptown)

The American Museum of Natural History, Central Park West and 79th Street, is one of the most amazing museums in the entire world! With 22 connecting buildings located on 23 acres of land and with 343 million objects and 41 exhibition halls, you could spend months, even years, exploring.

If you only have a few hours to spare, you might want to take a guided "highlights" tour. It lasts about an hour. You'll pick up facts like snakes have no eyelids and reptiles keep growing their entire lives and only stop when they die. It's also handy to know that a Reticulated Python can swallow an entire deer whole and that's dinner for eight months.

Don't miss the world's largest collection of dinosaur bones on the fourth floor. You'll find reconstructed skeletons of *Brontosaurus*, *Stegosaurus*, and *Tyrannosaurus rex*.

You'll find yourself wondering why the dinosaurs became extinct after ruling the earth for 150 million years. We humans have only been around for about 30,000 years in our present form. Scientists haven't been able to piece together the dinosaur puzzle. One theory has to do with cataclysm and meteorites that changed

The Blue Whale is the largest animal that ever lived. Even its tongue weighs 3 tons (more than a Volkswagen Beetle). But they're very gentle mammals, and it's important that we protect them and other sea creatures from becoming extinct.

43

Tyrannosaurus rex
*(known as Rex to his/her
friends) had teeth 6
inches long and a mouth
that opened 4 feet wide
and a head that weighed
as much as one thousand
pounds. Can you imagine
how Rex felt with a
headache!*

Did you know a duckbill
Trachondontus *had 2,000
teeth!*

the earth's atmosphere. Another theory is
that flowering plants began to flourish, which
was good for mammals and bad for dinosaurs.
Why do you think the dinosaurs disappeared,
and what color do you think they were?

Besides dinosaurs, there are the fossilized
teeth of a giant extinct relative of the Great
White Shark which measured 45 feet long when
he/she was swimming around the ocean. And
then there are the Komodo Dragons from
Indonesia, and the slice of sequoia that's
1,342,000 years old, and the tortoise who E.T.'s
face was modeled from, and then, and then, and
then, and then!

The Museum of Natural History also offers
the **Naturemax Cinema**. This is no ordinary
movie house. The Naturemax screen rises 4
stories high and 66 feet wide. You'll ride the
rapids or surf gigantic, humongous waves where
you can hang ten. Movies are under one hour,
and they're a great way to rest your weary feet.

Stargazers! **The Hayden Planetarium**, at the
museum, offers "armchair" travelers a galactic
voyage. More than 100 projectors beam
"astro-nomical" constellations in the domed
theater. Shows are frequent and fascinating and
they'll leave you starry-eyed.

After all that museum exercise, drop in at the
Food Express for eats, quick and cheap. **The
American Museum Restaurant** is much more
expensive and someone probably needs a credit
card.

You might find the **flea market** around 76th
Street (near the Museum of Natural History).
But if you miss that one, ask around. New
Yorkers will send you to the "best of fleas" to buy
shoes, hats, or antiques.

Central Park *is the centerpiece of Manhattan and one of the world's great parks. The park took 16 years to complete, from 1857 to 1873.*

Whether you want to ice-skate, ride horses, go boating, or just plain people watch, Central Park is THE place to be.

1) **Sheep Meadow**-*Great for people watching or frisbees on sunny days.*
2) **Wollman Rink**-*Ice skating in winter is great here!*
3) **The Zoo**-*It's a nice size, recently fixed up, and you'll see penguins and polar bears.*
4) **Tavern on the Green**
5) **Strawberry Fields**-*Yoko Ono Lennon restored this tear-shaped garden in memory of John Lennon, her husband and famous musician who was assassinated in December 1980.*
6) **Loeb Boathouse**-*You can rent a rowboat and oar to your heart's content.*
7) **Belvedere Castle**-*Terrific for imagination adventures.*
8) **Conservatory Water**-*Where model boat races begin each warm Saturday, 10 a.m.*
9) **Carousel**
10) **Shakespeare Theater**-*Shakespeare in the park is great for a tear or a belly laugh, depending on the play and your mood.*
11) **Claremont Stables**-*The only stable left for park-crazy equestrians.*

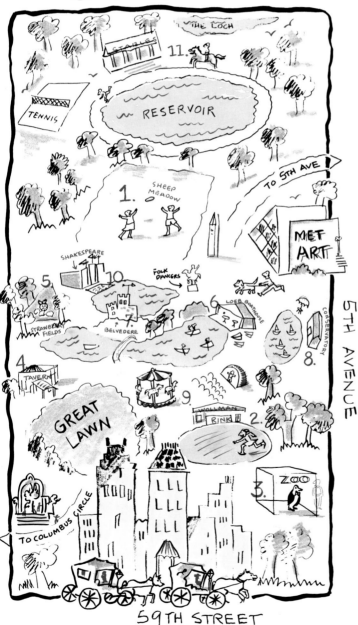

*When **Lincoln Center** was in the planning stages, the architects studied the rear-end size of average Americans. So they could sit down in comfort, of course.*

Lincoln Center is a gigantic performance complex, eight separate buildings clustered around a plaza. Sometimes you can catch terrific outdoor entertainment here, so keep your ears and eyes open. When you visit Lincoln Center during the day, it's a good idea to take a "behind-the-scenes" tour. They start downstairs at the **Metropolitan Opera House** and you'll also see the **New York State Theater** and **Avery Fisher Hall**. When you're on tour, see if you can catch a rehearsal-in-progress. Better yet, come to the opera, the ballet, or the symphony.

At 2 Columbus Circle make a stop at the **New York Convention and Visitors Bureau**. That's where you find all the news about what's happening in the city right at the moment.

You better believe **Zabar's** is unbelievable. It's sort of a deli, sort of a market, sort of gourmet, sort of . . . never mind. Never has food looked so weird and wonderful. You'll have trouble identifying certain things hanging from the ceiling, packed into the shelves, or displayed in the coolers. Zabar's is the best and can't be explained, so go and see for yourself on Broadway.

While you're on the Upper West Side, if you need some fifties flash to parade around in, or any other vintage apparel, don't pass up **Alice Underground** on Columbus and 78th Street. The clothes are clean, look new, and there are tons of them. Great for costumes, exotica, and just plain wear.

Almost next door, **Mythology** stocks flying birds, funny cards, Japanese comic books, and unique toys.

A "reel" good place to catch a movie is **Loew's Theater** on 84th and Broadway. It's clean and nice with great video games and good movies.

Fifth Avenue! Well, what about it? It's the symbol of chic and sophistication. It borders Central Park on the east side. You'll see museums, shops, and fancy-pants high-rises all on one street. There are lots of great bookstores and the window-shopping comes cheap.

At the **Jewish Museum** you'll see the archaeological discoveries from biblical Israel and children's drawings from the Holocaust. This

It's a bird, it's a plane, it's a pooch patrol! Since so many people work all day in New York City and they don't have front or back yards, they hire dog walkers. You guessed it, those are folks who walk dogs for a living. It's fun to follow these doggy herds for a few minutes and imagine what would happen if a cat ran by.

*Where can you find a complete Egyptian temple in a giant atrium? Where else but at the **Metropolitan Museum of Art**. The Temple of Dendur, in the Sackler Wing, was a gift from the government of Egypt in 1965. You'll have no problem imagining an oasis in the desert or a camel trip past Abydos and Thebes all the way to Dendur.*

wonderful museum provides a perspective of Jewish history and rich cultural heritage.

The Metropolitan Museum offers special walking tours that include the Japanese Galleries, the European Rooms, and Museum Highlights. If you're into armor, steel yourself. The Met has gigantic suits of medieval armor as well as kid-sized armor that belonged to squires, the assistants to the knights. You almost forgot the firearm collection. There are knives that turn into guns and guns that turn into canes. And don't overstep the main steps to the Met. Buy a hot dog or a soft pretzel and hang out. The people watching is unbeatable.

Skate on over to **The Ice Studio**, on Lexington Avenue between 73rd and 74th, any time of year when you're ready for some chills and thrills. You can take lessons or free skate your figure eights at this indoor ice rink. If you've got an appetite for something more substantial after all that skating, give **Ray's Pizza** a try. There's one on Third Avenue at 77th Street. Say cheese.

Yorkville, on the Upper East Side, is New York's German-American community. Munch on sausage, sauerkraut, and fabulous pastries. You'll discover Hungarian and Czech establishments also. Czech it out.

*You absolutely must climb to the top of the **Guggenheim** even if you think you hate modern art.*

49

11. Cloisters, Cathedrals, and Gospel

The famous ***Apollo Theater*** *in Harlem is where many black entertainers got their start. These days it's been renovated and you can still catch a rising star on Wednesday talent nights.*

arlem (from about 110th to 178th Street and between Park and Morningside avenues and the Harlem and Hudson rivers above Morningside Park) boasts a fascinating history. General George Washington had his headquarters here during the Revolutionary War at the Morris-Jumel Mansion. At the end of the nineteenth century, Harlem was a very fashionable neighborhood. There were Germans, then came the Irish, and then Jewish and Italian immigrants. After 1900, blacks started moving into Harlem from Lower Manhattan, the American South, and the West Indies.

Harlem became a hot spot during the 1920s and early 1930s with lots of fancy clubs, great jazz musicians, dancers, and other artists. But then Harlem fell on hard times. Recently, it has had a resurgence. Buppies fixed up historic townhouses and whole neighborhoods have gone from funky to fabulous. But the crack (cocaine) problem in many parts of Harlem, just like other cities, means you need to be careful where you

go. One of the best ways to see Harlem is on tour. Companies to choose from include Harlem Spirituals, Inc., Harlem Your Way!, and Harlem Renaissance Tours, among others.

Harlem Spirituals, Inc., offers gospel tours. Go to church on Sunday morning and then feast on a succulent soul food breakfast at the famous **Sylvia's**.

Harlem Your Way! offers highlights on foot along with music, gallery, and soul food tours.

History and "Taste of Harlem" food tours and theater specials may be arranged through **Harlem Renaissance Tours**.

The Cathedral Church of St. John the Divine (on Amsterdam and 112th) can hold as many as ten thousand people at once. Started in 1892, the cathedral still has plenty of work to be done. Many young apprentices are working on it now, carving and cutting stone in the tradition of European master craftspeople.

On the way to Spanish Harlem, visit the **Museum of the City of New York**, on Fifth Avenue, which is just that—a museum all about New York City. You'll find dioramas of the days when the Algonquin Indians roamed the forests and models of Dutch forts, complete with cannons. The third floor is really terrific for toys, including a tiny enchanted palace "made of leaves and twigs and magic" and a Humpty Dumpty Circus. If these sound like they're just for little kids, guess again. But you'll also find Period Rooms, a Costume Gallery, and even the story of the first mailman who saddled it to Boston.

Northeast of Central Park (between Park Avenue and the East River above E. 96th Street) is

Graffiti as Art—Some artists learned their craft with spray cans on the walls and now they're famous.

Spanish Harlem. It's a neighborhood in transition with the wealth of the Upper East Side pressing into its boundaries. Lots of different types of people live here—you could call it an ethnic salsa. Spanish Harlem is a tough area, so be careful where you go.

At **El Museo del Barrio** (The Neighborhood Museum), on Fifth Avenue, you can examine the permanent collection of santos (carved wooden saints) and pre-Columbian artifacts as well as an array of changing exhibitions. Some of the best Latin American and Puerto Rican artists are represented.

Journey back into the days of gray stone castles, knights, abbots, and kings. All you have to do is travel uptown to **The Cloisters** in Fort Tryon Park. High on the hill, you'll imagine what it was like to live in the twelfth to fifteenth centuries before people knew there was a big world out there. The gardens at the Cloisters are filled with flowers and spices. The building is made of actual European cloisters, chapels, and other structures, brought over stone by stone. The famous Unicorn Tapestry might make you dream of mythical beasts. And take a close look at the Unicorn chalice, said to be made from the horn of that very shy beast. Rainy days are especially good for atmosphere, but please travel during daylight hours only! Catch the #4 Municipal bus at 34th and Madison Avenue for a mini-tour of the neighborhoods. The bus stops right in front of the Cloisters.

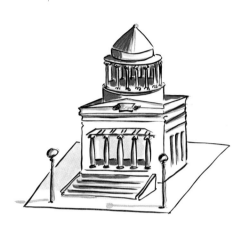

On the way to the Cloisters, you'll pass **Grant's Tomb**. *Have you ever wondered who's buried in Grant's Tomb?* (*General Grant, the Civil War hero, and his horse*)

12. The Babe, Baboons, and Other Boroughs

The **Bronx** is the only borough of New York City that's situated on the mainland. It is the home of **Yankee Stadium**. Remember Babe Ruth? He was one of the most famous hitters of all time. Other Yankee greats include Lou Gehrig, Joe DiMaggio, and Mickey Mantle. The Yankees have played here since 1923, and the stadium was given a major overhaul in the mid-1970s. If it's baseball season and you're a fan, buy yourself a hotdog and a Yankee cap and get ready for the 7th inning stretch. Go to a day game and also see the old neighborhoods from a different era.

Bronx Park sits almost in the center of this borough. Here you'll find two famous nature stops, the **Bronx Zoo** and the **New York Botanical Garden**. The Botanical Garden is great for strolling and sniffing. You can't cover all 250 acres in one day so aim for the rose gardens or rhododendron valley.

If you thrill to the call of the wild, the Bronx Zoo is the place for you. You'll find more than 4,000 wild animals grazing, snoozing, and swinging in 265 acres of forests, fields, and jungles. All the habitats are designed to look like the real thing. You can take the Bengali Express monorail train and safari to the wildest forests of

*What do bats and Australian bushbabies have in common? The World of Darkness at the **Bronx Zoo**. There you can see night turned into day and all these nocturnal creatures happily going about their business.*

Asia (2 miles worth). Elephants, Siberian tigers, and rhinoceroses are all doing their thing.

The rare and endangered Snow Leopard from remote regions of the Himalayas roam the Himalayan Highlands. And then there's Jungle World or the Children's Zoo where you do as the animals do — try out your own turtle shell or climb a spider's web.

The Safari Train is the easiest (and laziest) way to enjoy the Bronx Zoo. All you have to do is sit and ooh and ah.

Brooklyn is big! It's got the most people of all the boroughs. In fact, if Brooklyn were a city all by itself, it would be the fifth-largest city in the United States. Just like Manhattan, Brooklyn's neighborhoods are filled with all varieties of people: black, Italian, Jewish, Greek, Scandinavian, Polish, Middle Eastern, and Caribbean.

Brooklyn Heights is one of the better areas in the borough and the location of several places to explore. Meander **Atlantic Avenue** for a touch of the Middle East. Shops and stores come in exotic flavors like the spices and foods you'll find there. On the **Brooklyn Heights Promenade**, you'll catch one of the best scenic overlooks of New York. Watch the tugboats bringing in big ships and barges bringing in the fuel that keeps the lights burning in the city. Giant cruise liners pass by on their way to and from distant ports. Look out at Ellis Island or Governor's Island where the U.S. Coast Guard keeps its boats.

The Brooklyn Museum is world famous, but it's one of the least crowded museums in the New York area. If you're curious about how folks used to live in America, head straight for the fourth floor. You can wander through a planta-

tion house dating from 1730 or a New England home from the 1800s, and there's a house that was built in Brooklyn in 1675, walls and all. When you think about it, a house inside a museum is pretty weird.

The third floor gives Egyptian buffs the chance to examine sarcophogi (tombs) and jewelry (they had pierced ears back then) dating from ancient Egypt. Then there's the outdoor sculpture garden with a twist and the museum café with real food.

The Brooklyn Botanical Garden is home to 12,000 plants. Originally a waste dump, these fifty acres were reclaimed in 1910—fabulous! The Visitor's Center has a brochure to tell you what's blooming when you're there. In the Fragrance Garden, all the plants are labeled in braille. Try closing your eyes and letting your friend lead you around by your nose.

In the Shakespeare Garden, you'll find out that Maria said, "Get ye all three into a box tree" in Twelfth Night. So get ye to Shakespeare's Garden.

Brooklyn Children's Museum, Brooklyn Avenue at St. Mark's Avenue, is handy for hands-on fun. The front door is a giant sewer pipe.

*Many Indians from the Mohawk tribe worked on the bridges spanning the East River. It was very dangerous, high-wire work, but that didn't bother the Mohawks who were integral in bridge creation. The **Brooklyn Bridge** is a suspension bridge held up by cables that form matrixes and "spiderweb" patterns. So look up as much as you look down and around. For a walk on the bridge, start at City Hall Park and cross Park Row to the pedestrian lane and arrive at Cadman Plaza West, Brooklyn Heights.*

Inside, you'll learn about nature, science, and space. Get ready to roll up your sleeves and dig in.

BAM isn't a weird food, a caveman buzzword, or a new club. It's the **Brooklyn Academy of Music** (on Lafayette Ave.) and you need to find out what the score is. Shows are varied and wonderful, from an Italian Puppet Theater presenting the Wizard of Oz to Chinese Golden Dragon Acrobats and Magicians. Programs change all the time, so do yourself a favor and check in with BAM ASAP!

You've probably seen **Coney Island**'s famous boardwalk on celluloid. It's been around a long time.

*Is **Coney Island** an island? No! Does Coney Island have great hot dogs? Yes! They're famous and now you can buy them in other states in the U.S., but why not bite into the "real thing" at **Nathan's**. They usually come with onions and sauerkraut and lots of goop. **Astroland Amusement Park** boasts one of the world's super roller coasters, the Cyclone.*

Photo courtesy of New York Convention & Visitors Bureau

56

These days it's a little seedy, but you can still gorge on cotton candy, saltwater taffy, and all the cokes you need for a very upset tummy!

You'll also find the **New York Aquarium** on Coney Island. Gentle, graceful (they weigh two tons!), and funny-looking beluga whales will entertain you with leaps and dives. You might spot a toadfish or a triggerfish. And then there's the 90,000-gallon shark tank with all those ominous-looking teeth.

Queens is 109 square miles and named after an English queen. Over a million people live here in distinctly different neighborhoods.

One of them, **Astoria**, is among the largest Greek neighborhoods in the world. You'll also find many Italians tucked into this corner of Queens. This is your chance to tour the neighborhood markets and fruit stands and put together an international (and delicious!) lunch. Try a different market for each course. How about some salami, french bread, or mortadella? And don't forget dessert! Homemade baklava (with all that honey and nuts and butter), a few slices of cheese (there are hundreds to choose from), and finally, gelato (ices) served in a paper cup.

Movie buffs can "roll 'em!" at the **American Museum of the Moving Image**. Located in a 1920s studio in Astoria, AMMI is the only museum in the U.S. entirely devoted to film and television. If you've ever wondered what a best boy or a key grip does in movieland, AMMI's "Behind the Scene" exhibit is the place to find out. There's also lights, camera, action, when you mix your own soundtrack or transform into Rocky or Marilyn Monroe via a magic mirror. With a neo-Egyptian film palace installation, 60,000 film artifacts, historical and state-of-the-

BAM! BAM! POW!

techie-art equipment, you'll find yourself in cinema-tech heaven.

Flushing Meadows-Corona Park, where the 1939 and 1964 World's Fairs were both held, now offers a variety of sights: Queens Zoo, Queens Botanical Gardens, Queens Museum, the New York Hall of Science, and the USTA National Tennis Center, where the U.S. Open is held.

Have you ever wondered how light bends? Or what atoms look like? Or why the World Trade Center doesn't fall down? Well, the **New York Hall of Science**, in Queens, holds the answers to these questions and plenty more. It's a fabulous high-tech museum and it's great even if you've always thought you couldn't understand science. It's all hands-on, so you should bounce, poof, grow, or shrink, all for the sake of science.

Staten Island is much more than a ferry ride. It's a little bit of country in a big city where you can hike, horseback ride, or picnic. **Richmond-town Restoration** lets you wander through 17th, 18th, and 19th century streets for a feel of America's past. There's even the oldest "one-room" schoolhouse remaining in America, dating from 1695.

On the 80 acres of Snug Harbor, you'll discover the award-winning **Staten Island Children's Museum** with lots of action-packed exhibits, a botanical garden, and probably a concert, art exhibit, or special event.

Staten Island Tibetan Art holds a major collection of Tibetan bronzes, thankas, and paintings. Meditate on the Chinese, Japanese, Nepalese, and Indian artworks. If you're interested in non-Western art, history, and thought, this is nirvana.

Roller Coaster
Coney Island

58

13. "Say good-bye, Kong"

N ow that the trip is over, what are you going to take home with you? Well, you'll definitely have lots of souvenirs. Maybe a Statue of Liberty hat or a MOMA T-shirt or even a new haircut. And you probably took snapshots. Those come in handy to show friends and family what you saw and did. Maybe you made a new friend, a New Yorker who shared her or his city with you. But most of all, you'll take your memories and your thoughts about what travel is all about: new experiences, foreign sights and sounds, people and places very different from you and your own life. Travel isn't always easy or comfortable, but it's the best way to open yourself to the whole world. If you kept a travel notebook, make sure you tuck it somewhere safe and reread it next year or the year after that. It's always amazing to see how much you change as you grow. And how the city can change from one visit to the next. You'll want to come back to the "Big Apple" because you can never see all there is to see in one bite!

Events: What's Happening in New York City

Dates are subject to change. Call the New York Convention & Visitors Bureau, Inc., at 212-397-8222 for specific dates and times.

January/New Year's Eve
Fireworks and midnight run, Central Park
Ball drops at Times Square
Fireworks, Prospect Park, Brooklyn

February
Chinese New Year's Celebration
Empire State Building Run-up
Ice Capades, Madison Square Garden

March
Central Park Egg-Rolling Contest, Great Lawn, Central Park
St. Patrick's Day Parade, Fifth Ave.
Easter Parade, Fifth Ave.

April
Baseball Season begins
Meadowfair, children's festival, Snug Harbor Cultural Center, Staten Island

May
Solidarity Day Parade, Fifth Ave.
SoHo Festival, Prince Street, West Broadway—Sixth Ave.
Cherry Blossom Weekend, Brooklyn Botanical Garden
Fabulous Fifth Avenue Fair, Brooklyn
Martin Luther King, Jr., Parade, Fifth Ave.
Memorial Day Parade

June
Free Metropolitan Opera concerts in the parks
Museum Mile Festival, Fifth Ave.
Puerto Rican Day parade, Fifth Ave.
Lower East Side Jewish Festival, East Broadway, Clinton-Essex Sts.

July
Festa Italiana
Free Summerpier concerts at South Street Seaport
Free Summergarden concerts at Museum of Modern Art
Free Shakespeare Festival in Central Park
Macy's Fourth of July Fireworks

August
Free New York Philharmonic concerts in the parks, five boroughs
Greenwich Village Jazz Festival
Elephant Weekend, Bronx Zoo

September
Feast of San Gennaro, Little Italy
Schooner Regatta, South Street Seaport
Labor Day Parade, Fifth Ave.

October
Hispanic Day Parade, Fifth Ave.
Columbus Day Parade, Fifth Ave.
Haunted Greenhouse, New York Botanical Garden
Halloween Parade, Greenwich Village

November
Basketball Season begins
NYC Marathon, five-borough run
Children's Book Week, New York Public Library
Veterans Day Parade, Fifth Ave.
Macy's Thanksgiving Day Parade

Mid-November through early January
Radio City Music Hall Spectacular
Star of Christmas, Hayden Planetarium
Origami Holiday Tree, American Museum of Natural History
Animated store window displays, Fifth Ave.

December through early January
Giant Christmas Tree at Rockefeller Center
Giant Lighted Snowflake, Fifth Ave. at 57th St.
Christmas Tree and Baroque Crèche, Metropolitan Museum of Art

Appendix

Prices and hours are subject to frequent change. Many places are closed on holidays. Call first to double check information. Manhattan addresses unless otherwise indicated.

American Museum of Immigration
Statue of Liberty National Monument
Liberty Island, 212-363-3200
Ferry from Battery Park
Handicapped access

American Museum of Natural History
Central Park West at 79th St.
212-769-5100
Handicapped access

American Museum of the Moving Image
35th Ave. at 36th St., Astoria, Queens
718-784-0077

Astor Place Theatre
212-254-4370

AT&T InfoQuest
Madison Ave. (betw. 55th and 56th Sts.)
212-605-5500
Special tours for hearing impaired 212-605-6188

Bronx Zoo
Fordham Road and the Bronx River Parkway
212-367-1010
Handicapped access/wheelchairs available, call
    212-220-5188

Brooklyn Academy of Music
30 Lafayette Ave., Brooklyn
718-636-4100

Brooklyn Botanic Garden
1000 Washington Ave., Brooklyn
718-622-4544
Handicapped access

Brooklyn Children's Museum
145 Brooklyn Ave., Brooklyn
718-735-4400
Handicapped access

Brooklyn Museum
200 Eastern Parkway, Brooklyn
718-638-5000
Handicapped access

Carnegie Hall
154 W. 57th St.
212-247-7459

Castle Clinton
Battery Park
212-344-7220/264-8711
Handicapped access

Central Park
　Emergencies—Use call boxes in park to reach
    Central Park Police Precinct, look for bright
    colored phone design on box
　Handicapped parking permits—212-860-1842
　Lost and Found—212-397-3165
　Zoo—212-439-6500
　Wollman Rink—212-517-4800

Chrysler Building
Lexington Ave. and 42nd St.

Circle Line
Pier 83 at 42nd St.
212-563-3200

City Hall
212-566-5700
Handicapped access

Claremont Stables
175 West 89th St.
212-724-5100

Cloisters
Fort Tryon Park
212-923-3700, ext. 26
Handicapped access

Coney Island
Surf Ave. to W. 37th St., Brooklyn
718-946-1350

**Cooper Union for the Advancement of Science
and Art**
Astor Place at Lafayette St.

El Museo del Barrio
1230 Fifth Ave.
212-831-7272
Limited handicapped access

Ellis Island
By Ferry from Battery Park
212-269-5755

Empire State Building
Fifth Ave. at 34th St.
212-736-3100

Federal Hall Memorial Museum
15 Pine St.
212-264-8711

Federal Reserve
33 Liberty St. at Wall St.
Free Tour
Reservations at least 1 month in advance
212-720-6130

Flatiron Building
Fifth Ave., Broadway, and 23rd St.
on the corner

Fraunces Tavern
Broad and Pearl Streets

Gallery of Science and Art
IBM Building, 590 Madison Ave.
212-407-3500

Grand Central Terminal
E. 42nd St. betw. Vanderbilt and Lexington Aves.

Guggenheim
1071 Fifth Ave. (near 88th St.)
212-860-1313
Handicapped access

Guinness World Records Exhibit Hall
Empire State Building, 350 Fifth Ave.
212-947-2335
Limited handicapped access

Harlem Renaissance Tours
18 E. 105th St.
212-722-9534

Harlem Spirituals, Inc.
1457 Broadway, Room 1008
212-302-2594

Harlem Your Way!
129 W. 130th St.
212-690-1687

Hayden Planetarium
81st St. at Central Park West
212-769-5920

Horn & Hardart Automat
Third Ave. and 42nd St.
212-599-1665

Intrepid Sea-Air-Space Museum
Pier 86 on the Hudson River (W. 46th)
212-245-0072

Jewish Museum
1109 Fifth Avenue
212-860-1888
Handicapped access—call for appointment

Lincoln Center
Broadway between 62nd and 66th Sts.
212-877-1800

Metropolitan Museum of Art
Fifth Ave. and E. 82nd St.
212-879-5500

Museum of Broadcasting
1 East 53rd St.
212-752-7684

Museum of Colored Glass and Light
72 Wooster (betw. Broome and Spring Sts.)
Upstairs
212-226-7258

Museum of Holography
11 Mercer St.
212-925-0581

Museum of Modern Art
11 West 53rd St.
212-956-7070
Handicapped access

Museum of the City of New York
103rd St. and Fifth Ave.
212-534-1034
Handicapped access

Naturemax Theater
American Museum of Natural History
Central Park West at 79th St.
212-769-5650

NBC Studio Tours
RCA Building, 30 Rockefeller Center
Between Fifth and Sixth Aves., 50th St.
212-664-4000

New York Aquarium
West 8th St. Boardwalk, Brooklyn
718-266-8500

New York Botanical Garden
Bronx Park, Bronx
212-220-8700
Handicapped access

New York City Fire Museum
278 Spring (betw. Varick and Hudson)
212-691-1303

New York Convention and Visitors Bureau
2 Columbus Circle (59th & Broadway)
212-397-8222

New York Experience
McGraw-Hill Building, Rockefeller Center
1221 Sixth Ave. between 48th and 49th Sts.
212-869-0345

New York Hall of Science
47-10 111th St., Corona (Queens)
718-699-0005

New York Public Library
Fifth Ave. and 42nd St.
212-661-7220

New York Stock Exchange
Visitors Center, 20 Broad St., 3rd Fl.
212-623-5167/212-656-3000

Public Theatre
Lafayette St.
212-598-7100

Queens Botanical Garden
43-50 Main St., Flushing, Queens
718-886-3800

Queens Museum
New York City Bldg., Flushing Meadows, Queens
718-592-2405

Radio City Music Hall
Rockefeller Center

Richmondtown Restoration
Richmond Road, Staten Island
718-351-1617

Roosevelt Island Tramway
Second Ave. and East 60th St.

South Street Seaport
Pier 16, Pioneer Sail
212-669-9400

St. Patrick's Cathedral
Fifth Ave. between 50th and 51st Sts.

Staten Island Children's Museum
15 Beach St., Staten Island
718-273-2060

Staten Island Ferry
Battery Park and South Ferry
212-806-6940
Bay St., St. George, Staten Island
718-727-2508

Staten Island Zoo
614 Broadway, Staten Island
718-442-3101

Statue of Liberty
Liberty Island
Tours leave from Castle Clinton, Battery Park
212-260-5755
Handicapped access (not to crown)

Tibetan Museum
338 Lighthouse, Staten Island
718-987-4378

TKTS
Broadway and 47th St., 212-354-5800
2 World Trade Center, 212-354-5800

United Nations
First Ave. and East 46th St.
212-754-7713 or 963-4440

Vietnam Veterans Memorial
55 Water St.

World Trade Center
1 World Trade Center
212-466-4170

Yankee Stadium
The Bronx
212-293-6000

Kidding Around with John Muir Publications

We are making the world more accessible for young travelers. In your hand you have one of several John Muir Publications guides written and designed especially for kids. We will be *Kidding Around* other cities also. Send us your thoughts, corrections, and suggestions. We also publish other books about travel and other subjects. Let us know if you would like one of our catalogs.

TITLES NOW
AVAILABLE IN THE
SERIES

Kidding Around Atlanta
Kidding Around London
Kidding Around Los Angeles
Kidding Around New York City
Kidding Around San Francisco
Kidding Around Washington, D.C.

John Muir Publications
P.O. Box 613
Santa Fe, New Mexico 87504
(505) 982-4078